SCIENCE ANSWERS

Classification

FROM MAMMALS TO FUNGI

Louise and Richard Spilsbury

Heinemann
LIBRARY

www.heinemann.co.uk/library
Visit our website to find out more information about **Heinemann Library** books.

To order:
☎ Phone 44 (0) 1865 888066
🖹 Send a fax to 44 (0) 1865 314091
🖥 Visit the Heinemann Bookshop at www.heinemann.co.uk/library to browse our catalogue and order online.

First published in Great Britain by
Heinemann Library, Halley Court,
Jordan Hill, Oxford OX2 8EJ,
part of Harcourt Education.

Heinemann is a registered trademark of
Harcourt Education Ltd.

Editorial: Nancy Dickmann and Tanvi Rai
Design: Richard Parker and Celia Floyd
Illustrations: Wooden Ark
Picture Research: Rebecca Sodergren and
Pete Morris
Production: Séverine Ribierre

Originated by Dot Gradations Ltd
Printed in China by WKT
Company Limited

ISBN 0 431 17514 4
08 07 06 05 04
10 9 8 7 6 5 4 3 2 1

**British Library Cataloguing
in Publication Data**
Spilsbury, Louise and Richard
Classification. – (Science Answers)
570.1'2
A full catalogue record for this book is
available from the British Library.

Acknowledgements
The publishers would like to thank the
following for permission to reproduce
photographs: Corbis **p. 18**; Corbis/Gray
Hardel **p. 4**; FLPA/Chris Mattison **p. 13**;
Harcourt Education Ltd/Tudor Photography
pp. 7, 19; NHPA/ANT Photo Library **p. 23**;
NHPA/Christopher Ratier **p. 20**;
NHPA/Daniel Heuclin **p. 25**; NHPA/Daryl
Balfour **p. 27**; NHPA/David Woodfall
p. 15; NHPA/G J Cambridge **p. 17**;
NHPA/Norbert Wu **p. 6**; NHPA/Stephen
Dalton **pp. 16, 22, 26**; NHPA/Trevor
McDonald **p. 21**; Science Photo
Library/Carl Linnaeus **p. 28**; Science Photo
Library/Dr Tony Brain & Dr David Parker
p. 9; Science Photo Library/Eric Grave **p.
10**; Science Photo Library/Eye of Science **p.
12**; Science Photo Library/Jan Hinsch **p.
11**; Science Photo Library/Rudiger Lehnen
p. 29; SPL/Claude Nuridsany & Marie
Perennou **p. 24**; ZEFA **p. 8**.

Cover photograph of a cattle egret sitting
on an African elephant reproduced with
permission of FLPA/P. Hartman.

Every effort has been made to contact copyright
holders of any material reproduced in this book. Any
omissions will be rectified in subsequent printings if
notice is given to the publishers.

The paper used to print these books comes from
sustainable resources.

Contents

Any words appearing in bold, **like this**, are explained in the Glossary.

About the experiments and demonstrations

This book contains some boxes headed 'Science Answers'. Each one describes an experiment or demonstration that you can try yourself. There are some simple safety rules to follow when doing an experiment:

- Ask an adult to help with any cutting using a sharp knife.
- Always wash your hands with soap after handling plant or animal material.

Materials you will use

Most of the experiments and demonstrations in this book can be done with objects/foods that you can find at home or buy cheaply from a shop. You will also need a pencil and paper to record results.

What is classification?

Classification is the way people make some sense of the complicated world we live in. We arrange things into groups according to their similarities and differences. For example, we classify when we tidy up toys into boxes or put books away in alphabetical order in a library.

Classifying life

Living things have several **life processes** in common – such as growth, **respiration** and **reproduction** – but can be as different as a cactus and a shark. We classify living things partly based on their appearance. For example, any animal with feathers is a bird. However, although some creatures such as birds and bats look similar in shape, they are very different. This is why we classify partly on the way they live – for example, whether they lay eggs or not. Some differences between **organisms** are very small, so classification can be tricky.

A variety of life

There is a huge variety of living beings in nature. Sometimes it is possible to find lots of different sorts of life co-existing in the same natural surroundings, as in tropical forests or deep in the sea, near the ocean floor. Classifying and naming the different living things on Earth is called taxonomy.

Kingdoms of life

There are an estimated 10 million different **species** of livings things on Earth. Up until the 20th century, scientists divided organisms into two big groups, called **kingdoms**. Today, most scientists agree that living things should be classified into five kingdoms. These are named bacteria, protists, fungi, plants and animals. The members of each kingdom share similar features.

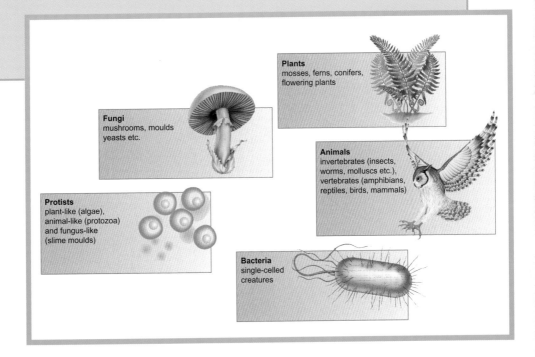

Plants
mosses, ferns, conifers, flowering plants

Fungi
mushrooms, moulds yeasts etc.

Animals
invertebrates (insects, worms, molluscs etc.), vertebrates (amphibians, reptiles, birds, mammals)

Protists
plant-like (algae), animal-like (protozoa) and fungus-like (slime moulds)

Bacteria
single-celled creatures

Classification over time

- Early humans classified the plants or animals they found as either safe or harmful.
- Around 2300 years ago, the Greek philosopher Aristotle classified some organisms by their insides – for example whether they had blood or not – and how they behaved.
- In the 18th century, the Swedish **botanist** Linnaeus developed a system for classifying any living thing.
- Scientists today classify using Linnaeus's system plus more recent information, such as the types of **cell** inside an organism's body.

Classification groupings

Within each kingdom, organisms are divided up into large subgroups, usually called **phyla**. Each phylum is divided into smaller groups with shared features called classes. Classes are divided into smaller groups called orders, orders into families, families into **genera** and genera into species. A species is a single kind of organism. The members of a species are very similar and can usually reproduce together.

Universal species

Mountain lion, puma and cougar are different names for the same species of big cat. To avoid confusion, every species is given a double name. The double names are written in Latin, the language widely understood when Linnaeus developed his classification system. *Felis concolor* describes the same big cat. *Felis* is the genus – rather like a family name – and *concolor* is the individual species name.

Similar but not the same

Some animals, such as dolphins and fish, look similar but are classified into different groups. Although this bottlenosed dolphin lives in water and looks like a fish, it is actually a **mammal** like us.

INVESTIGATION: Sorting into groups

Have a go at classifying some objects!

EQUIPMENT:
A mixed box of different sized, shaped and coloured sweets;
a bag of peanuts in shells; two large sheets of paper; pens.

INVESTIGATION STEPS:
1 Take a sheet of paper and tip the sweets on to it.
2 Divide the sweets into groups containing similar features.
   You can sort them by colour, shape or whether they are
   hard or soft.
3 Draw circles around the different sets. Some sweets will
   fall into more than one pile, depending on how you
   choose to sort them.
4 Next repeat steps 1 and 2 for the peanuts. You may have
   to use different features to sort them – for example,
   length. Then break open
   each shell – how many
   nuts are there inside?

CONCLUSION:
Factory-made sweets are
easier to classify than
peanuts, because their
differences and similarities
are more obvious.
Sometimes, however, it is
necessary to classify using
hidden features, when
things look similar from
the outside. Classification
takes time!

What are bacteria?

Bacteria, which make up one the five **kingdoms**, are the simplest **independent** living things on Earth. Billions of them live in water, soil, air and on or in other **organisms**. Bacteria are classified by the shapes of their **cells**. For example, some are round, some are rod-shaped, while others are corkscrew-shaped.

Simple cells

Cells are the building blocks of all living things. Bacteria usually live as single cells or chains of identical cells. Most cells contain a distinct part called a **nucleus**, which helps control the **life processes** in the cell. Bacteria are classified together partly because they have no nucleus.

Helpful bacteria

Many animals rely on bacteria in their stomachs to help them digest food. When we eat yoghurt (like the girl in the picture), we top up the bacteria in our stomachs. Natural live yoghurt contains bacteria like *Lactobacillus acidophilus*, which protects our **digestive** tract and helps in **digestion**. Other bacteria are used to make foods such as cheese, or vital medicines.

Tiny life

Bacteria are too small to see without a powerful microscope. This magnified (made bigger) photo shows thousands of rod-shaped orange bacteria on the tip of a household pin!

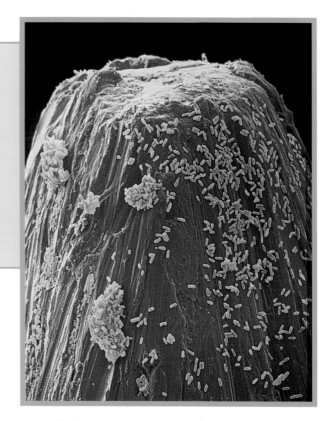

Harmful bacteria

Some bacteria are harmful to other organisms. They affect life processes, usually by producing damaging toxins (poisons). Bacteria **reproduce** very quickly in the right conditions. This can mean illnesses and dangerous diseases can spread quickly. For example, if *Meningococcus* bacteria get into the brain, they can rapidly cause meningitis.

Cyanobacteria

Cyanobacteria (we say 'sigh-anno') are a special kind of bacteria that have existed for billions of years. They use energy from sunlight to make their own food. Plants also use this process, which is called **photosynthesis**.

Cyanobacteria often live in groups called colonies. Some colonies live amongst the roots of plants and help plants get the **nutrients** they need. Some live on bare wet rock or concrete. Others live in extreme conditions, such as hot springs. Although the water is rich in nutrients, these tough cyanobacteria have to cope with temperatures up to 75 °C. In contrast, red cyanobacteria live in the freezing snow of Antarctica.

What are protists?

The protist **kingdom** groups together single-celled **organisms** that can only be seen under a microscope and live in water. Protists differ from bacteria by having a distinct **nucleus**.

Consumers

Some protists are rather like tiny animals, because they move around to find and consume food, rather than making it themselves as plants do. Some protists, such as amoebas, move by stretching out part of their **cell** wall. Their liquid body flows into the new space created. Others have a long hair that they wave back and forth to swim along, a bit like the fins and tail of a fish.

Protists use different ways to get a meal. *Vorticella* has an opening in the top of its cell, which is surrounded by tiny hairs. When it beats the hairs in water, it creates a kind of whirlpool that funnels floating food into its body.

Catching a meal

Amoebas move around **prey** such as a bacterium or another, smaller protist to trap it before **digesting** it. In this picture the amoeba is surrounding its prey using cell wall extensions. When it is fully enclosed it will be swallowed and digested within a cavity in the amoeba.

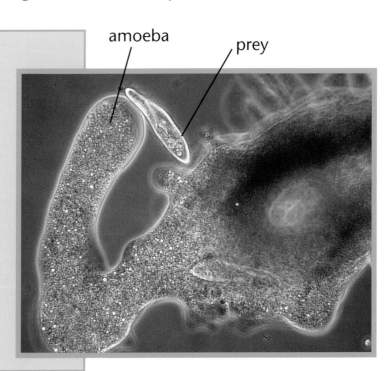

amoeba

prey

Producers

Some protists are a bit like tiny plants, because they produce their own food using **photosynthesis**. Protists in the world's oceans make up the major part of **plankton**. **Oxygen**, created as a waste product of photosynthesis by the protists living in plankton, is vital for **respiration** in marine animals. What is more, plankton is a vital food for fish and other animals that live in the water.

Diatoms are protists with two hard shells that look like they are made of glass. Their shells form boxes around their bodies, in different shapes such as stars or circles.

Colourful creatures

Diatoms are very distinctive protists, with 10,000 different **species**, each having intricate patterns, colours and shapes.

What are fungi?

The fungi **kingdom** groups together living things such as mushrooms, toadstools and yeast. Yeasts, mildews, moulds and rusts are tiny single-**celled** fungi. Larger fungi such as mushrooms, puffballs and toadstools are made up of many different cells.

Hidden fungi

Many fungi are made up of a network of cotton-like threads called **hyphae** (we say 'hi-fee'). Hyphae grow through materials such as damp soil and wood, which are foods for fungi. Their cells make special chemicals that dissolve the food. The hyphae then take in the released **nutrients**.

Hyphae are usually hidden. The bits of fungi we can see are just used to **reproduce**, using **spores**. Spores are like tiny, tough seeds. The thin flaps on the underside of a mushroom's wide cap are where its spores are made. When the spores ripen, they may fall, blow or wash somewhere with the right growing conditions and develop into new fungi.

spore-producing body   hyphae

Parts of a fungus

This magnified photo of fungus *Aspergillus fumigatus* shows how a fungus is structured. It is made up of a thread-like hyphae (grey) and spore-producing fruiting bodies (brown).

Decomposers

Many fungi break down dead **organisms** as they feed. This is called **decomposition**. Some fungi feed on dead wood and leaves, which are full of useful nutrients. They absorb some of the nutrients from these, and the rest wash into the ground. This makes the soil fertile, helping different plants to grow.

Tree recycling

Fungi are very important decomposers of dead organisms. They remove their nutrients and change them into a form that other living organisms can then use. This picture shows bracket fungi growing on fallen wood in a forest in Monteverde, Costa Rica.

Many fungi grow hyphae into and among tree roots. Some of the nutrients their hyphae take in from the soil enter the trees' roots as well. In return, some of the sugar in the roots, which the trees make by **photosynthesis**, is absorbed by the hyphae. This kind of relationship that benefits both living things (here, the fungi and plants) is called **symbiosis**.

No benefit

Some fungi are **parasites** – they feed on other living things without providing anything useful in return. For example, the condition 'athlete's foot' is caused by a fungus that lives on human skin, making the skin flake and itch.

What are plants?

Plants are one of the best-known **kingdoms** of living things. All plants can make their own food inside their bodies. They do this by **photosynthesis**. In this process, plants use **energy** from sunlight to combine water and carbon dioxide (a gas in the air) to create food, in the form of sugars. Their ability to produce their own food is what sets plants apart from other kingdoms, such as animals and fungi.

Plant divisions

Even though all plants are able to photosynthesize, there are many different kinds of plants. The simplest way of grouping them is to look at their structures; in particular, by the way they take in water and **nutrients** – whether they are **vascular** or **nonvascular**.

Parts of a vascular flowering plant

Photosynthesis happens mostly in plant leaves. The flowers are used for **reproduction** and they make seeds (stored in fruits). Stems hold up the other parts of the plant. Roots fix the plant in the ground and take in water and nutrients from the soil.

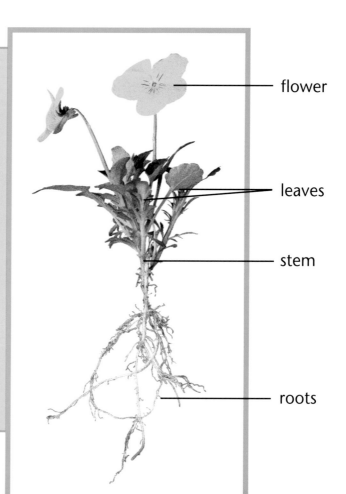

flower

leaves

stem

roots

What are vascular plants?

Vascular plants carry water, nutrients and food around their bodies in a series of tubes. They take in water and dissolved nutrients from the soil through their roots. The water is taken from the roots through tubes to the stems and leaves. Sugars that are made in the leaves are then carried to other parts by tubes too. The tubes in vascular plants are all connected together, rather like the blood vessels inside the human body.

How do plant tubes work?

Vascular plants have two kinds of tubes. Xylem (we say 'zy-lum') tubes carry water and nutrients taken in from soil from the roots to the other parts of the plant. Phloem (we say 'flo-em') tubes carry the sugars made in the leaves by photosynthesis to the other parts of the plant. The plant uses all these things to help it grow.

Vascular heights

Most of the plants in the world are vascular plants. Vascular plants like these beech trees grow tall because their tubes carry water and nutrients up and down the plant.

Vascular plant groups

Vascular plants can be divided into three different groups: flowering plants; conifers; and ferns and their relatives, the clubmosses and horsetails. Flowering plants reproduce using seeds made in flowers. Conifers make seeds too, but in **cones** rather than flowers. The ferns and their relatives reproduce using **spores**.

How do flowers work?

For a seed to grow in a flowering plant, pollen from a male part of a flower has to join with an egg in the female part. This is called pollination. The female part can be in the same flower or a different one. Some flowers attract insects or birds to eat their **nectar**. As they feed, the visitors also pick up pollen, which they transfer to other flowers. Other flowering plants use the wind to spread their pollen to other plants.

Scent attractions

Honeysuckle flowers smell strongest in the evenings. The scent attracts moths, which fly at night, to feed on their nectar and transfer their pollen to other flowers.

What are conifers like?

Conifers have two types of cones on their branches that are used for reproduction. The smaller male cones produce pollen that blows on to larger female cones. Once pollinated, seeds develop inside the female cones. These cones fall or open up to release the seeds when they are ready. Most conifers have leaves shaped like needles and they are **evergreens**. They gradually shed and replace leaves all year round, not all at once in autumn, so they always look green.

Fern spores

The patches on the underside of these fern fronds are clusters of spores, which may grow into new fern plants when they fall.

Ferns, clubmosses and horsetails

The plants in this third group of vascular plants reproduce using spores. Their water-carrying tubes are found in the walls of their hollow stems. There are about 12,500 different **species** of ferns. Ferns have leaf-like parts called fronds and most grow from underground stems. Clubmosses look a bit like mosses, whereas horsetails have distinctive circles of thin leaves around their stems.

What are nonvascular plants?

Nonvascular plants do not have tubes. They usually get the water and nutrients they need by growing in damp places. The different parts of the plants, such as leaves, absorb (take in) the water they need from their surroundings. Nonvascular plants can be divided into two groups: mosses and liverworts, and algae. In the woodland in this picture, mosses grow on the trees and algae live in the water.

Mosses and liverworts

Mosses and liverworts have leaves, stems and roots. They live on damp walls, roofs or rocks, and on fallen trees. Moss grows in groups, forming spongy green cushions. Liverworts also live together in groups and they have small, flat green leaves. Both reproduce using spores.

Algae

Algae have no leaves, stems or roots. Some algae consist of a single **cell**, but others, such as seaweed, have large fronds. Small algae reproduce by dividing cells. Larger algae, such as kelp, reproduce using spores.

DEMONSTRATION: Leaf classification

EQUIPMENT:
Ten different tree leaves – can be fallen leaves, or cuttings (for example, hedge trimmings) given by someone with a garden, or photos of leaves on trees; paper and pencil.

DEMONSTRATION STEPS:
1 Study the leaves to see what differences and similarities they have. Think about these things as you do so. Are the leaves like tiny pointed scales? Are they needle-shaped, or wide? If wide, are they simple (single leaf) or compound leaves (groups of smaller leaves on one stalk)?
2 Sort the leaves into groups according to the differences you identify. Write down the details of the different groups. You can even draw out some leaf shapes to study the variation.

EXPLANATION:
Trees are classified partly according to leaf shape. Trees with needle-like or scale leaves are conifers. For example, pine trees have needles, whereas cedar trees have scales. Other leaf shapes are found on broad-leaved trees. Single broad leaves, such as oak or holly, are called

simple. Leaves made up of groups of smaller leaves are called compound. Compound leaves are found on trees such as ash and rowan. Use a tree identification book to identify tree species more closely.

What are animals?

The animal **kingdom** groups together **organisms** as different as whales and jellyfish. However different, all animals are made of many **cells** and get all the **energy** they need to live by consuming (taking in) food. Most animals can move at some stage in their life. Many sense and react to the world using nerves and muscles controlled by a brain.

How are animals classified?

Animals are usually grouped based on how they support and protect their bodies. Most **species** of animals in the world are **invertebrates** – they have no internal bony skeleton. Invertebrates use other ways to keep their body shape. For example, worms use their body's muscles and fluids, while crabs use a hard outer shell.

Only about 3 per cent of all animals are **vertebrates** – they have backbones and internal skeletons. There are five different classes (groups) of vertebrates: fish, reptiles (such as lizards), amphibians (such as frogs), birds and mammals.

Animal consumers

Most animals get food by consuming other organisms. Some of them, like this cheetah, rely on speed to catch their **prey**.

Which animals are invertebrates?

Invertebrates range in size from tiny worms made of fewer than 1000 **cells** to giant squids as long as a bus. They are divided into around 30 **phyla**. These include sea urchins and starfish, worms, sponges and the following groups.

Molluscs

Squids, octopuses, clams and mussels are all types of molluscs. Many molluscs have a spiky tongue for grating food. Their soft bodies may be protected by a chalky shell, as in snails, or a slimy outer skin, as in slugs.

Sea anemones, corals and jellyfish

These belong to one group because they have special stinging cells on their **tentacles** to catch food and protect themselves from attack. Corals live together in vast groups on the sea floor. The chalky or rubbery skeletons they make to live in are what make up reefs.

How do anemones feed?

A sea anemone can attach itself to rocks or coral. Its tentacles are arranged in a ring around its mouth. It waits for its food to swim past, stings it with its tentacles and then pushes it into its mouth.

Arthropods

Arthropods are invertebrates such as insects, millipedes, lobsters and scorpions. They have a tough, plastic-like skeleton on the outside of their bodies. Their bodies are divided into sections and their legs have joints so that they can bend. As arthropods get bigger, they grow out of their skeletons. They then have to **moult** to get rid of the old shell and replace it with a new, bigger one!

Deadly jab

Scorpions use the stingers on their tails to inject poison into their prey. This stops it from moving as they eat it alive!

How many legs?

One way of grouping different arthropods is by the number of body parts or legs that they have. For example, all adult insects have three body sections and six legs. Spiders and scorpions both have two body sections and eight legs, but differ in how they catch **prey**. Spiders make sticky webs out of silk, in which their prey becomes caught. Scorpions use large claws at the front of their legs and a sting on their tail.

How are fish and frogs different?

Fish and frogs are both **vertebrates** that hatch from soft eggs in water. Fish spend their whole lives in water. Frogs are amphibians – animals that spend the early part of their life in water but live mainly on land as adults.

What are fish?

Some fish live in the sea, some in rivers or lakes, and others move from one to the other. Fish breathe using parts called gills, which take in **oxygen** dissolved in the water. They swim by moving their body from side to side, using fins for control. Fish skin is usually covered with **scales**, which fit together like tiles on a roof. Young fish eat tiny plants, insect eggs or **larvae**. Adult fish eat **plankton**, plants, smaller fish or other animals.

Fishy facts

There is a huge range of fish in the world. The *Pandalea pygmaea* fish from the Phillipines is only 13 millimetres long when fully grown. On the other hand, whale sharks, like this one, measure about 12–19 metres long!

What are amphibians like?

Frogs, toads, newts and salamanders are all amphibians. Adult amphibians have soft, moist skin without scales. They are **cold-blooded**, which means that they cannot warm themselves up and their bodies stay the same temperature as their surroundings. Young amphibians that hatch from eggs (amphibian larvae) look completely different to adult amphibians. As they develop, they undergo huge changes in a process called **metamorphosis**.

Frog metamorphosis

Female frogs lay hundreds of eggs under water. Tadpoles hatch out of these eggs. Tadpoles have long tails for swimming, and breathe using gills. They eat bits of plants using tiny teeth. As they grow, tadpoles develop legs so they can walk on land, and their tails get much smaller (notice the short, stumpy tail in the picture). Young frogs leave the water to live on land about four months after hatching. Adult frogs have lungs so that they can breathe air, and they eat small animals that they catch with a sticky tongue.

What are reptiles and birds?

There are many similarities between reptiles and birds. To reproduce, both kinds of animal lay hard or leathery eggs on land, usually in nests. The eggs' shells protect the babies inside from drying up. This allows reptiles and birds to live in drier places than animals such as amphibians. There are also some important differences between reptiles and birds.

What are reptiles like?

Reptiles have skin covered with **scales**, and most reptiles have teeth. There are four different groups of reptiles. Snakes have long bodies and no legs. Crocodiles and alligators have long jaws, long tails and short legs. Lizards are similar to crocodiles and alligators, but have shorter heads. Turtles and tortoises have bodies protected by bony, box-shaped shells.

From small to big

When reptiles, like this baby grass snake, hatch out of their leathery eggs, they look like tiny versions of their parents. Most can look after themselves straight away.

What is special about birds?

Birds are the only living things to have skin covered with feathers. All birds have wings, which most **species** use for flying. Birds do not have teeth. They catch their food using a hard beak or the claws on their feet. Birds usually lay their eggs in nests. There is a huge variety of birds on Earth, from tiny hummingbirds only 6 centimetres long, to giant ostriches almost 3 metres tall!

Finding food

Birds eat a variety of foods and find it in different ways. Many birds feed during the day, but owls have large eyes and hunt at night for small animals such as mice. Hummingbirds beat their wings quickly to hover over flowers as they suck up **nectar**. Pelicans have a big pouch-like throat, which they use to scoop up fish from water.

Where do birds live?

Birds live in all parts of the world. This colourful macaw lives in the Amazonian rainforest.

How do we classify mammals?

Mammals can look as different as flying bats, tree-living gibbons, diving whales and us – humans! However, they all have several things in common.

Mammals are all **vertebrates** that have hair on some or all of their bodies. They are **warm-blooded** – they change their inside temperature depending on whether it is hot or cold outside. All mammals breathe air through lungs. Female mammals can suckle their babies – feed them on milk from their bodies.

Mother's milk

Most baby mammals, like this young giraffe, suckle milk from teats on their mother's belly or chest.

Unusual mammals

Most mammal young develop inside their mothers. However, female marsupials, such as kangaroos and possums, give birth to tiny undeveloped young. Their young usually develop in a pouch on the mother's outside. Meanwhile, platypuses are mammals that lay eggs which contain their young. Their babies suckle once they have hatched.

People who found the answers

Aristotle (384–322 BC)

Aristotle was a teacher, writer and philosopher in Ancient Greece. His new ways of thinking influenced many different areas of study, including biology. Aristotle was the first to classify animals by their way of life – for example, whether or not they had blood or laid eggs – or by how they were made up. For example, he worked out that dolphins are not fish, although they look similar. His work influenced scientists for hundreds of years after his death.

Karl von Linné (known as Linnaeus) (1707–78)

Linnaeus (pictured here) was a Swedish **naturalist** and **botanist**. In 1735, he published his *Systema Naturae*. This was a universal system for classifying life on Earth. It could be used by any scientist who could speak or read Latin. This included his way of giving any **organism** a double name, showing its **species** and also what it is grouped with. Linnaeus's system is still used today.

Amazing facts

- The chemical that keeps the feathers of African flamingos pink results from them eating lots of red cyanobacteria. The green colour of slow-moving **mammals** called sloths is because of the tiny **photosynthetic** protists that live in their fur!

- One fungus in Oregon, USA, covers nearly 10 square kilometres (6.2 square miles) – about 1600 football fields – beneath the pine forest floor. The honey fungus may have lived on this site for over 8000 years.

- There are over half a million **species** of beetle. That is one in every four species of animal on Earth.

- Although there are only 8000 species of ant, there are so many individual ants that together they weigh one-tenth of all animals put together!

- Some ocean snails live at depths of 4 kilometres (2.5 miles).

- The giant clam (below) can reach 1.4 metres long and weigh over 300 kilograms.

Glossary

botanist plant scientist

cells building blocks of living things, so small they can only be seen with a microscope. Most plants and animals are made up of millions of cells.

cold-blooded describes animals that cannot warm themselves up. Their bodies stay the same temperature as their surroundings.

cones form of dry fruit in which conifer seeds develop. Cones are often egg-shaped with overlapping woody scales.

decomposition breaking down chemically, rotting away

digestion breaking down of food we eat into nutrients that the body can absorb and use for energy

digestive to do with digestion

energy the power that all living things need in order to live, grow and do everything that they do

evergreen describes trees that lose and replace a few leaves all year round, rather than losing all their leaves in winter, as deciduous trees do

genus (plural **genera**) classification grouping. Each genus is divided into species.

hyphae thread-like parts fungi grow and use to take in nutrients

independent describes organisms that can move around on their own

invertebrates animals without backbones

kingdoms name for the five groups that living things are divided into: plants, animals, fungi, protists and bacteria

larvae young of certain animals that look very different from their parents and must undergo metamorphosis before they become adults, egs. caterpillars into butterflies, tadpoles into frogs.

life processes activities that all living things must do to live and thrive

mammals group of animals that includes humans. All mammals feed their babies milk from their own bodies and have some hair.

metamorphosis change in body shape that happens in some kinds of animals as they change from young animals into adults

moult to shed feathers, hair or skin. When an insect moults it sheds its hard outer skeleton in order to grow bigger.

naturalist person who studies plants and animals

nectar sugary substance that plants make to attract insects and birds, which eat it

nonvascular describes an organism that does not have veins or tubes in its body

nucleus part of a cell that helps control the life processes within the cell

nutrients chemicals that plants and animals need in order to live

organism living thing

oxygen gas in the air around us which living things need in order to live

parasite creature that lives on or in another living creature and takes its food from it without giving any benefit in return

photosynthesis process by which plants make their own food using carbon dioxide, water and energy from sunlight

phylum (plural **phyla**) classification grouping. Each phylum is divided into classes.

plankton microscopic organisms that live in the surface waters of the oceans

prey animal that is caught and eaten by another animal

reproduction/reproduce when a living thing produces young like itself

respiration process by which living things release energy from their food

scales overlapping or interlocking pieces that form a protective layer over reptile and fish skin

species class of organisms that have similar characteristics

spores tiny particles, which some organisms produce, that can eventually grow into a new organism like the parent

symbiosis partnership between two living things from which both members benefit

tentacles long, thin 'feelers' that stick out from an animal's body

vascular describes an organism that has veins or tubes in its body

vertebrates animals with backbones

warm-blooded describes animals that can warm up or cool down when the surrounding temperature changes

Index

More books to read

Cells & Life: The Diversity of Life, Robert Snedden
(Heinemann Library, 2002)
Classifying Living Things series, Richard and Louise Spilsbury and
Andrew Solway (Heinemann Library, 2003)
Nature Encyclopedia (Dorling Kindersley, 1998)

Titles in the *Science Answers* series include:

Hardback   0 431 17512 8

Hardback   0 431 17513 6

Hardback   0 431 17514 4

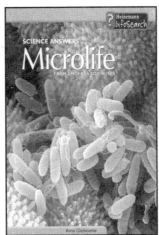

Hardback   0 431 17515 2

Hardback   0 431 17516 0

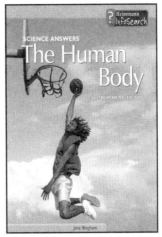

Hardback   0 431 17517 9

Find out about the other titles in this series on our website www.heinemann.co.uk/library